Cornerstones of Freedom

The Story of
THE
BARBARY
PIRATES

By R. Conrad Stein

Illustrated by Tom Dunnington

ST. MATHIAS LIBRARY
CHICAGO, ILLINOIS

 CHILDRENS PRESS, CHICAGO

Library of Congress Cataloging in Publication Data

Stein, R. Conrad.
  The story of the Barbary pirates.

  (Cornerstones of freedom)
  Summary: Relates the circumstances of the
United States' involvement with the Barbary
States of North Africa in the early years of
the nineteenth century.
  1.   United States—History—Tripolitan War,
1801-1805—Juvenile literature.   [1.   United
States—History—Tripolitan War, 1801-1805]
I.   Dunnington, Tom, ill.   II.   Title.
III.   Series.
E335.S83   973.4   82-4436
ISBN 0-516-04632-2   AACR2

Copyright © 1982 by Regensteiner Publishing Enterprises, Inc.
All rights reserved. Published simultaneously in Canada.
Printed in the United States of America.

In 1801 a warship cut through the waters of the
Mediterranean Sea. The ship flew a British flag, but
it really was the American schooner *Enterprise*. She
was commanded by Lieutenant Andrew Sterett. On
the horizon Sterett saw a speck. He wheeled his ship
to investigate.

Lieutenant Sterett discovered the speck to be a
pirate ship called the *Tripoli*. She was one of many
pirate ships that sailed out of the Barbary States of
North Africa. Because the *Enterprise* flew a British
flag, the two ships drew close to each other without
firing. Great Britain and the Barbary pirates were
at peace. The young American nation, however, was
fighting the pirates.

Sterett studied the pirate ship. She was as big as his vessel. She also carried fourteen guns — two more than the *Enterprise* had. Still Sterett believed he could beat the pirates in a fight — as long as he did not let his ship get too close to the enemy vessel. The Barbary pirates' favorite method of fighting was to board an opposing vessel. Once on board, they were deadly fighters with their cutlasses. But American sailors were more skilled at gunnery than were the pirates.

When the two ships were within shouting distance, Sterett asked the pirate captain where he was going. The pirate, seeing the British flag, thought the *Enterprise* was a British ship. He answered that he was looking for American ships to attack. He was disappointed because he had been at sea for days and had yet to see one.

Sterett immediately ordered his riflemen to open fire on the pirate ship. He then brought down the British flag. In its place he ran up the American colors. The surprised pirate captain shouted to his crew to man their guns. One of the early battles in America's war with the Barbary pirates broke out.

Both ships blasted at each other with their can-

non. Several times the pirate captain turned his ship sharply. He was trying to draw close to the *Enterprise* so his men could board the ship. Skillfully Sterett kept the *Enterprise* just the right distance from the *Tripoli*. He stayed far enough away to prevent the pirates from jumping aboard. But he stayed close enough to pound the *Tripoli* with his cannon.

The fight lasted three hours. In those days a cannon duel between ships required expert seamanship

and knowledge of gunnery. A ship captain had to know how to take advantage of the wind and every little ripple of the sea. Sailing ships tilted as they maneuvered. And when the ships tilted, their guns tilted, too. A skilled captain could maneuver his ship to aim at an enemy's ship while the enemy's guns were tilted either toward the water or into the sky. A sailing-ship captain also tried to cross an opponent's bow or stern. In that position he could hit the other ship with all his broadside cannon while the enemy vessel was unable to return fire. The maneuver was called *raking*.

Round after round of Sterett's cannonballs ripped into the pirate ship. Dead and wounded pirates lay sprawled on the *Tripoli's* deck. The *Tripoli's* mainmast had been knocked down. It rested on her deck like a fallen tree. Hardly any pirate cannonballs had struck the *Enterprise*. American officers had learned gunnery from the British. And the British were the greatest seamen in the world. The Barbary pirates soon would learn to respect the fighting ships of the American Navy.

The *Tripoli* finally surrendered to Lieutenant Sterett and the *Enterprise*. The Americans had scored an impressive victory. But it would take more than one victory to win this war. It would take money, determination, and lives. But the young American nation was determined to defeat the Barbary pirates.

The Barbary pirates operated mainly from four North African nations: Morocco, Algiers, Tunis, and Tripoli. Today Algiers, Tunis, and Tripoli are the nations of Algeria, Tunisia, and Libya. The rulers of the old Barbary States worked in league with bands of pirates. The pirates attacked merchant ships in the Mediterranean. They captured the ships, stole their cargo, and held the passengers and crew for ransom. The rulers of the Barbary States demanded payment from other countries for "protection" from the pirates. Nations wishing to trade in the Mediterranean had to pay or see their vessels attacked.

For hundreds of years the Barbary States had forced European countries to make protection payments. Even England paid the Barbary States. Surely the British had the naval might to crush the pirates. Still England chose to pay. Historians believe that Britain wanted the pirates to operate so they could weaken Britain's trading rivals.

The rulers of the Barbary States were untrustworthy. Often they accepted payments from a country one day, and attacked that country's merchant ships the next.

In 1783 a new nation began trading in the Mediterranean. The Americans had goods to sell, and they were excellent sailors. While America was still a colony, the British paid her protection fees. Now the new country had to deal with the North African pirates on her own. The Americans had to decide whether to pay or to fight.

One American who believed in fighting the pirates was Thomas Jefferson. While George Washington was president, Jefferson wrote: "Tribute or

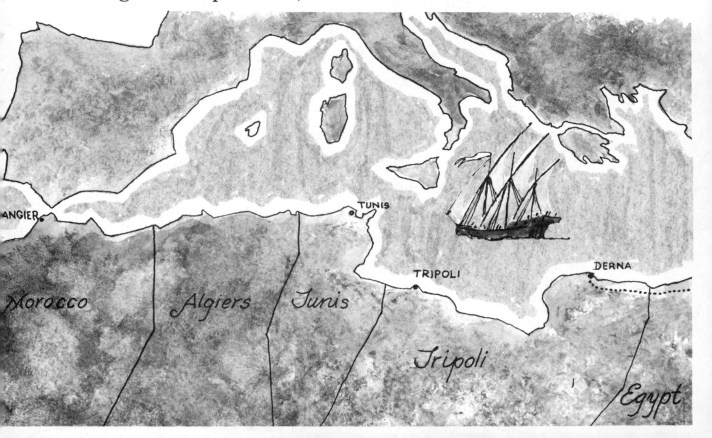

ANGIER

TUNIS

TRIPOLI

DERNA

Morocco   Algiers   Tunis

Tripoli

Egypt

war is the usual alternative of these Barbary States. Why not build a navy and decide on war? We cannot begin in a better cause or against a better foe." This was an unusual stand for Jefferson to take. He did not believe in war. He later ran for the presidency on the platform "Peace is our passion." Yet the actions of the pirates so angered Jefferson that he was driven to prepare for war.

Another American who urged war against the Barbary States was William Eaton. Eaton would later lead an amazing attack against a pirate stronghold. In 1798, however, his job was to try to negotiate treaties with the Barbary leaders he hated. Of the Barbary chiefs Eaton said, "There is not a scoundrel among them, from the prince to the muleteer, who will not beg and steal."

But in the United States many American Congressmen believed it would be cheaper to pay the pirates than to go to war with them. To go to war the United States would have to build ships and pay sailors. That would be too great an expense for so young a nation. So, until 1800, the United States chose to pay rather than fight the Barbary pirates.

Congress soon discovered, however, that the more they paid the greedier the Barbary pirates became.

In 1793 the Algerian chief asked for about forty thousand dollars to return some American sailors he had captured. Three years later, that same chief demanded a million dollars for a treaty. Morocco wanted money plus American guns and gunpowder. Other Barbary States wanted money, cannons, and ships. Some pirate leaders asked for personal gifts such as jewelry and gold watches.

By 1800 the United States had paid the Barbary states two million dollars in cash and other "gifts" for their leaders. Still the Barbary chiefs were not satisfied. In 1801 the leader of Tripoli demanded even larger payments. The United States refused. The Tripoli chief chopped down the flagpole that flew the American flag over his capital city. With that act, Tripoli had declared war against the United States.

The newly elected president, Thomas Jefferson, was furious over Tripoli's declaration of war. Earlier Congress had voted funds to build a small but hard-hitting navy. Jefferson sent that new navy to the Mediterranean. The United States never officially declared war against the Barbary States. Nevertheless, a war raged along the coast of North Africa for the next four years.

The Americans enjoyed early success in the war. But their fleet was unable to stop completely the raids of the Barbary pirates. Then two events occurred that changed the nature of the war. One was the arrival of several new, powerful ships. The second was a remarkable land invasion led by William Eaton. In 1801 a new American fleet entered the Mediterranean Sea. Leading the fleet were two superb warships—the frigates *Philadelphia* and *Constitution*. The Americans had learned the art of shipbuilding from the British. Their new warships were both sturdy and swift. The *Constitution* was later nicknamed "Old Ironsides" because enemy cannonballs seemed to bounce off her thick sides. This historic ship is now displayed at the harbor in Boston.

All the ships in the new American fleet bristled with guns. The *Constitution* had forty-four guns. The *Philadelphia* had thirty-eight. Completing the American flotilla were several schooners. Each of those was armed with fourteen to sixteen guns.

Commanding this new navy was an ill-tempered but brave captain named Edward Preble. Preble was a veteran of the Revolutionary War. He demanded perfection from all his men. At first he

ST. MATTHIAS LIBRARY
CHICAGO, ILLINOIS

was dismayed because not one of his officers was more than thirty years old. "A pack of boys," Preble called them. And, at the start of the campaign, his officers feared and disliked their commander.

The fleet stopped first at the Moroccan port of Tangier. The Moroccan chief had demanded more protection money. Preble lined up his ships outside the port. He told his gunners to take aim at the huge castle whose walls dominated the city. Preble was rowed toward the castle in a small boat manned by sailors. There he was to have a meeting with the high chief of Tangier. Preble had left written orders

ST. MATHIAS LIBRARY
CHICAGO, ILLINOIS

to be carried out if he did not return in proper time. The fleet was to bombard the castle, "regardless of my personal safety."

At the castle Preble refused to surrender his pistol. He also refused to kneel while talking to the chief, as was customary. Instead he demanded that Moroccan pirates cease their attacks on American ships. Perhaps the Moroccan chief had looked out his castle window and counted the guns pointed at his city. He promised Preble that American ships would have no more trouble with Moroccan pirates. Preble returned to his fleet in triumph. At last a North

ST. SEBASTIAN SCHOOL
ST. MATHIAS LIBRARY
8110 WELLINGTON
CHICAGO, ILLINOIS 60657

African leader had backed down to American naval might. Preble's personal bravery also had won the respect of his younger officers.

For many months the American fleet cruised the waters off North Africa. The warships protected merchant vessels, hunted pirates, and blockaded pirate ports. Then, at Tripoli, disaster struck. The mighty frigate *Philadelphia* ran aground just a few hundred yards from a pirate stronghold. The frigate became hopelessly stuck in the mud. A horde of sword-wielding pirates swooped toward it. The *Philadelphia's* captain tried to sink his ship by chopping holes in the bottom. But he did not have time. The captain was forced to surrender. Suddenly the pirates of Tripoli owned a mighty warship.

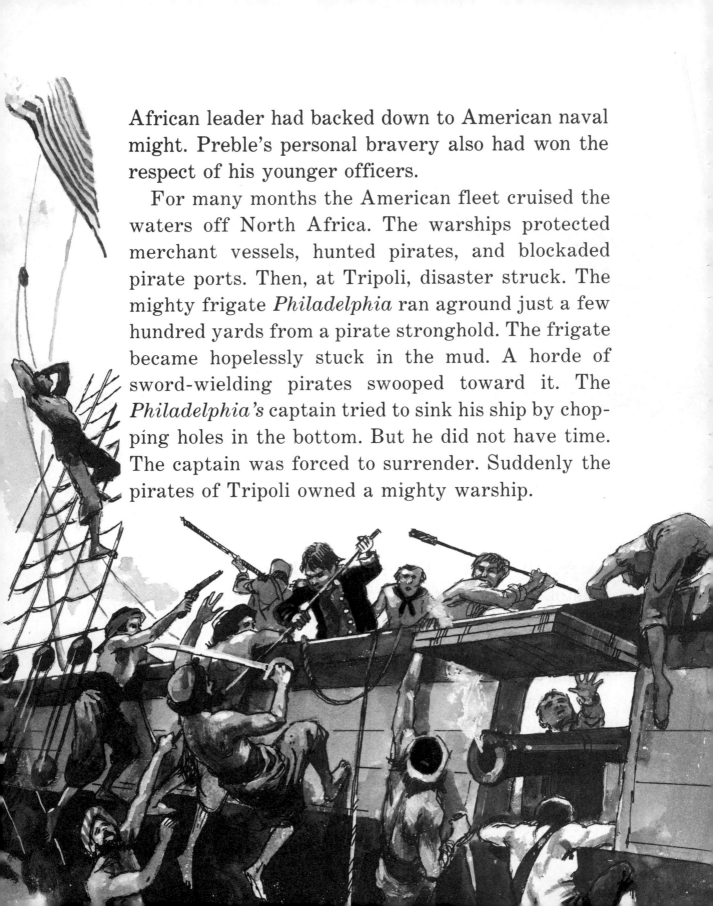

Preble was stunned at the turn of events. With the *Philadelphia* on their side, the pirates now had the power to defeat his fleet. The pirates had moved the *Philadelphia* into Tripoli harbor. Somehow Preble had to destroy the huge frigate. Preble knew he could not sail headlong into the harbor. The harbor guns, combined with the guns on the *Philadelphia*, could sink his entire fleet. There had to be another way to destroy the captured ship. The crafty old commander had a plan.

On a moonlit night an ancient freighter crept into Tripoli harbor. She was flying a British flag. The freighter was a former pirate ship that had been captured by the Americans. On her deck stood several American sailors and a Sicilian pilot. The Sicilian spoke Arabic and knew the North African coast. He had volunteered to come on the mission. He hoped to go to America one day.

The American sailors were not in uniform. Instead they were dressed as North African merchants. The freighter looked like a run-down cargo ship on a regular cruise. But crouched below her decks were nine American officers, about fifty sailors, and eight marines. They planned to destroy the *Philadelphia*. It would have been impossible to tow the huge frigate out to sea. So the raiders would sneak up on her, board her, overpower her pirate crew, set her on fire, and somehow escape.

At sea, miles away from Tripoli, Captain Preble nervously paced the deck of his ship. An officer named Decatur was in charge of the attack. Preble wondered if Decatur or any of his other young officers could carry out such a daring raid.

In Tripoli harbor the ancient freighter inched up to the *Philadelphia*. The frigate rested at anchor. From her deck a pirate watchmen challenged the freighter. "Who are you? What is your business?" Decatur whispered an answer to the Sicilian pilot. The Sicilian answered in Arabic that their freighter had come from Malta. He said they had lost their anchor in a storm. Could they please tie their ship alongside the *Philadelphia* until daybreak? Just then a sudden wind pushed the freighter close to the side of the *Philadelphia*. The watchman spotted an anchor tied to the freighter. "Americans!" the watchman shouted.

It was too late. American sailors and marines swarmed out of the hold and leaped aboard the *Philadelphia*. An officer named Charles Morris later wrote this account about the battle for the

Philadelphia: "In a moment we were near enough and the order, 'Board!' was given; and with this cry our men were soon on the decks of the frigate. The surprise had been complete. . . and the enemy made scarcely a show of resistance. A few were killed, one was made prisoner, and the remainder leaped overboard."

Immediately the attacking sailors set fires on the deck of the *Philadelphia.* The fires curled up the masts and crackled into the sails. Decatur ordered his men to jump back onto the freighter. He was the last to leave the deck of the blazing frigate. On the freighter, men scrambled down ropes to board two large rowboats. Those boats would tow the freighter out of the harbor.

The men in the small boats rowed desperately. Behind them the *Philadelphia* was a roaring inferno. The towering fire turned night into day. Cannons on the walls of Tripoli blasted at the freighter that was being towed slowly out of the harbor. Miraculously, the freighter escaped, unhit by the cannon fire.

When Decatur's men rejoined the fleet they were greeted warmly by Captain Preble. The tough old captain finally realized that his officers were not "a pack of boys." They had succeeded in what seemed to be an impossible raid. Preble recommended that Decatur be promoted to the rank of captain.

Around the world other seamen were amazed by Decatur's success. In England, the famous sea captain Lord Nelson called it "the most bold and daring act of the age." In the United States, Congress awarded medals to some of Decatur's men. And Congress also awarded American citizenship to the brave Sicilian pilot who had been so vital to the mission's success.

But as incredible as Decatur's raid was, the most amazing action during the Barbary wars was yet to come.

William Eaton was an unlikely man to become an American hero. Born in a small town in Connecticut, he ran away from home at the age of sixteen. Eaton was a big, rugged boy. He joined the state militia and saw action during the Revolutionary War. He later attended Dartmouth College, though he dropped out before graduating. Eaton became an officer in the American Army, but was dismissed because he had difficulty obeying orders. He was unemployed when a friend stepped in to help. The friend gained Eaton an appointment as America's representative to the Barbary States.

In North Africa Eaton quickly realized that the Barbary leaders were nothing more than a pack of thieves. He thought it was shameful that his government was paying the Barbary pirates for protection. Even so, Eaton's duties included the task of delivering gifts from the United States to the Barbary leaders.

Some of the "presents" Eaton had to bring to the chief of Tunis in the years before the Barbary wars were the following:

1 Fusee (musket) mounted with gold, set with diamonds
4 pair of pistols, mounted with gold
1 diamond ring

1 gold repeating watch with diamonds
1 gold snuffbox, set with diamonds
6 pieces of brocade gold
30 pieces superfine cloth of different colors
6 pieces satin, different colors

Eaton believed that war was the only way to stop this blackmail.

President Thomas Jefferson approved a plan Eaton had devised for deposing the leader of Tripoli. Eaton thought he would be able to force the present Tripoli chief off his throne and replace him with his brother. The brother, Eaton believed, would be friendlier to the United States. Jefferson gave Eaton twenty thousand dollars to raise an army. With that money the adventure of William Eaton began.

First, Eaton had to find the chief's brother, Hamet. Eaton sailed to Alexandria, Egypt, where Hamet was said to live. Eaton discovered that Hamet was hiding from assassins sent out by his brother. He finally found Hamet living in a small village. The man was terrified of being killed. But Eaton promised Hamet that he would be protected and would become the leader of Tripoli.

Next Eaton used his twenty thousand dollars to recruit an army of four hundred Greek, Arab, and Turkish troops. They were men willing to fight for pay. The only regular troops serving with Eaton were eight marines under the command of Lieutenant Presley O'Bannon. That handful of marines did much to save Eaton's mission. American marines today sing "From the halls of Montezuma to *the shores of Tripoli.*" They are referring to that long-ago action in North Africa.

Eaton gathered his army and set out. The group would have to march nearly five hundred miles over the rugged North African desert. Eaton's army was truly a foreign legion. It was made up of men of a half-dozen different nationalities. Their only purpose in fighting was the lure of American dollars. Ninety of the men were the personal staff of Hamet. They included his bodyguards, servants, and slaves. Eaton's cavalry consisted of just over a hundred camels.

During every mile of the long march Eaton had to assert his leadership. Several times his soldiers were ready to desert. Only Eaton's strength and stubbornness forced the men to march on. At one point even Hamet himself lost heart and wanted to end the march. Eaton lined up his marines and other loyal troops and threatened to open fire on Hamet and his men. The march continued.

Even when his food and water were exhausted, Eaton urged his army on. Their destination was the desert port of Bomba. There the army was to be supplied by American ships. On April 12, 1805, Eaton wrote in his diary: "Marched twenty-five miles... neither water nor fuel. The residue of our rice issued today; but the troops were obliged to eat it without cooking." Finally the ragtag army reached Bomba and picked up new supplies from the American ship *Argus*.

Ten days later Eaton led his men to the walls of Derna, an important city in Tripoli. Rolling in the waves off Derna were three American gunboats. Eaton ordered the leader of Derna to surrender. The leader's reply was "My head or yours." The battle began.

Muskets cracked and cannons roared. The

American gunboats bombarded the city from the sea. The marines led a wild charge on the city's walls. Eaton later wrote about the actions of Lieutenant O'Bannon: "Mr. O'Bannon urged forward with his marines. . . passed through a shower of musketry from the walls of the houses, took possession of the battery; planted the American flag on its ramparts; and turned its guns on the enemy. . . . " Eaton himself was wounded while charging against "a host of savages more than ten to our one."

The battle was bloody, terrifying, and confusing. But finally the Americans held Derna. For the first time in history the American flag was raised victoriously over a fortress in the Old World.

The victory at Derna did not satisfy everyone, however. The American naval command decided that Hamet would be an untrustworthy leader. So the Americans allowed a pirate named Yusef to rule Derna. The very disappointed Hamet had to leave Tripoli. So did an equally disappointed William Eaton.

But because of his victory at Derna, Eaton became an overnight hero in the United States. Newspapers wrote stories about his bravery. Often, however, heroes are quickly forgotten. When Eaton returned to the United States, he began drinking. He told confusing stories about his victory in North Africa. After a while, few people listened to his stories. Eaton died in 1811. Most newspapers did not even report the death of this one-time hero.

By 1805 the United States' involvement in the Barbary wars had ended. The Americans made one last, and probably unnecessary, payment to Tripoli. They continued making small payments to some Barbary leaders for ten years. But because of their

victories, the Americans had obtained a very important peace treaty. According to Captain Preble, the peace treaty was "on more honorable terms than any other nation has ever been able to command."

Amazingly, the young United States had accomplished what the ancient European powers had failed to do. For hundreds of years the Barbary pirates had attacked merchant ships in the Mediterranean. Finally a new country had stood up to the pirates and had won freedom of the seas.

About the Author

R. Conrad Stein was born and grew up in Chicago. He enlisted in the Marine Corps at the age of eighteen and served for three years. He then attended the University of Illinois where he received a bachelor's degree in history. He later studied in Mexico, earning an advanced degree from the University of Guanajuato. Mr. Stein is the author of many other books, articles, and short stories written for young people.

To finance his education, Mr. Stein worked as a merchant seaman. He has always had an interest in ships and life at sea.

Mr. Stein now lives in Pennsylvania with his wife, Deborah Kent, who is also a writer of books for young readers.

About the Artist

Tom Dunnington divides his time between book illustration and wildlife painting. He has done many books for Childrens Press, as well as working on textbooks, and is a regular contributor to "Highlights for Children." Tom lives in Oak Park, Illinois.

ST. MATTHIAS SCHOOL
ST. CLARA'S LIBRARY
CHICAGO, ILLINOIS
810 W. WELLINGTON
CHICAGO, ILL. 60657